Years ago,

in a land of deserts and dreams, it came to pass that a decree was lost, then came back again.

Now a decree is a type of very ancient document with lots of curly wurly writing on it that says you've got to obey it, because if you don't, you get into all sorts of trouble. And the topic of this decree was that everyone throughout the vast Roman Empire, wherever they were living, had to go back to the place they and their family originally came from and sign a form. This is called bureaucracy, which begins with the letter 'b' as in boring, budgie, and buttons. So, because of this decree the whole Roman Empire was soon full of people on the move, all getting blisters and moaning about the heat, the flies, and their marathon journey.

There was a man called Joseph, who lived in the country town of Nazareth. Now, when I say country town, I don't mean as in antique shops, timbered pubs and four-wheel drives. More like . . . not much going on; more like the permanent smell of camel; more like quiet, some would say slow, rustic folk who would put a 'w' on the end of rolo. Joseph was a good man, a kind man, but someone who was seen as a bit of a flake. You see Joseph was engaged to a pregnant girl called Mary, but Joseph wasn't the father. In fact it was all rather a mystery who the father was.

Let me explain . . .
Mary had told Joseph that she'd had a visit from an angel – a hugely important, big, glowing angel, a double-decker of an angel – called Gabriel, who had told her that she had been chosen by God to give birth to a very special child. And before you could say liquorice torpedoes, Mary found that she was pregnant.

Now, as I said, Joseph was a very decent gentleman, and when Mary told him the news Joseph took it all very calmly. But there was only one word to describe the state of Joseph's brain – marzipan – and he went for a lie down and had a very long sleep.

While he was asleep he had a dream, and during that dream an angel, certainly a mate of Gabriel's, appeared to Joseph and started explaining this confusing rigmarole. The basic gist of all this cosmic gynaecology was that, yes, Mary was pregnant, the child was to be called Jesus, and the child was a gift from God to the world. Joseph was to marry Mary and – seeing this was an angel – this winged creature of good news and G-force had brought Joseph a stonking milky way . . . allegedly. Listen, stranger things have happened in dreams . . .

Joseph awoke from his sleep feeling clearer, less anxious, and with the taste of terrestrial sweetness on his lips. For dreams are more real than we think – especially this one.

The Sweet News of Christmas

Copyright 2001 Stewart Henderson & J. John

First published 2001 by Word Publishing,
9 Holdom Avenue, Bletchley, Milton Keynes, Bucks, MK1 1QR, UK

All rights reserved.
No part of this publication may be reproduced
or transmitted in any form or by any means,
electronic or mechanical, including photocopy, recording
or any information storage and retrieval system, without
permission in writing from the publisher.

1-86024-234-0

Cover and internal design by David Lund

Produced for Word Publishing by
Bookprint Creative Services, P.O. Box 827, BN21 3YJ, England.
Printed in Great Britain.

So, returning to all the decree business . . . Joseph and, the by now heavily pregnant, Mary had to travel from Nazareth down to Bethlehem, where Joseph's family came from. Over stony hills they travelled, which were crunchie under foot. Mary rode on the back of a plodding donkey, which when you're pregnant is no bed of roses.

They arrived at Bethlehem well after eight, and could they book a room, in a hotel? Could they fudge! I mean, the poor woman was pregnant, tired, and possibly craving truffles for all we know. The only place that could be found for them was a cattle shed – very hygienic, very Patients Charter – attached to an inn. And that was where the baby called Jesus, the King of Heaven, was born – this bounty of God, this unique child who knew and could name each galaxy and planet from Mars to Pluto. This miracle boy, who had many names like the Lion of Judah, came to us via the whiffy surroundings of a squelchy shed where cows ate and . . . erm . . . I think you get the drift – you certainly would if you spent the night there! Well, so far, so strange. And so we continue . . .

Nearby in a field there was a bunch of shepherds. Well, there they were, guarding

their sheep, when all of a sudden
another angel appears to them from out of
a bright, starburst night.

Now these shepherds were uncomplicated chaps. There was nothing they liked better than to sit round a roaring fire talking in their own dialect about life, work and family. So when this angel appeared they were way the other side of terrified. They screamed . . . they laughed . . . they screamed . . .

However, the angel was used to this kind of response – people gibbering and swooning and so on – it goes with the job. So the angel being pleasant said, and I paraphrase: 'Time out lads – stop being a pathetic bunch of munchies. I bring fantastic news . . . brilliant news . . . happy, bouncy news. A baby has been born in Bethlehem, a Saviour in a stall, God in a shawl. The news is making me rhyme. Anyone fancy a dime?'

And then, as if one angel wasn't spectacular enough, the whole night sky then became full of shining, other heavenly beings, singing the ancient songs of God in harmonies and notes never heard. It was the best time ever, in the whole of human history, to be a shepherd.

When this fantastic display was finished and the stunning song complete, the shepherds excitedly began comparing notes. Then one stood up and said: 'Right lads, last one to Bethlehem is a toffee crisp.' And away they raced.

So the shepherds went rushing off, full of excitement, and found the cattle stall. And there they discovered what every really wise person knows – angels always tell the truth: for there was Jesus with Mary and Joseph – a squashy little baby – helpless, vulnerable, his eyes as bright as planets.

Well, by now the shepherds were as happy as gorillas on a lorry of bananas. And they became the first century equivalent of the Internet. They went out telling everybody, and not in a whisper, that this glorious baby was the Message, the King of Meekness, the promised Saviour of the World.

Now the shepherds were not the only visitors to pay homage to Jesus. And here's where the story gets a bit worrying, to say the least.

In the district where Jesus was born there was a king called Herod. He was a very bad man: he was nasty; he was devious; he was very unpleasant. And he had a terrible temper. He was permanently on a short fuse. However, when necessary, he could be charming – like a fox is charming, if hosting a very grand barbecue to which he's only invited chickens.

Anyway, one day, a rather grand collection of gentlemen from the far away East arrived, wanting to know where they could find this baby that everyone was talking about. These unexpected visitors had come a long way. They'd crossed toblerone mountains over which the orange sun shone by day, whilst at night they followed a star in the sky.

And when they got to Bethlehem, where the star was at its brightest, they stopped and agreed this must be the place where the baby had recently been born: this baby who would grow to be a king. But a king like the world had never seen: no throne, no palace, no treasures, but just a rich heart of love for all humankind. A priceless present from God to us.

These grand gentlemen from the East were a real bunch of smarties. They were known as the 'Wise Men', on account of them being wise and . . . erm . . . men – although those two words don't necessarily always go together. But their wisdom received a further boost when they managed to pinpoint, through following a star, the exact place where Jesus was.

However, the scheming Herod was
furious. He may have been all
regal and Turkish delight in
public, but as far as he was
concerned, there was only one King, one VIP, one triple A
List Celebrity – and Herod was it. But, in private,
Herod was extremely dangerous. He would do
anything to remove anyone he regarded as a threat to
his power. He sat in his sumptuous stateroom
seething and plotting, grabbing handfuls of jelly babies
from a nearby bowl, and biting off their heads – a
terrible sign of what was to come.

Meanwhile, the Wise Men found themselves being
sent by Herod to find out exactly where Jesus was being
nursed. Herod had told them that he wanted to come and
worship this new King too, but that was a lie.

The Wise Men went off to pay homage to Jesus but,
thankfully, their senses hadn't turned completely to walnut
whip. After they had visited Jesus and brought him fabulous
and exotic gifts of gold, frankincense and
myrrh, they were then warned in a dream not
to report back to Herod, but to get sharpish back
to their own land.

And after they'd gone, Joseph too had another
dream in which an angel gave him a similar warning:
'Go . . . and go now. For, not to put too fine a point on it,

Herod is full of black magic and means Jesus great harm.' So, faithful Joseph, courageous Mary, and the miracle that is Jesus fled from Bethlehem to Egypt, where they became homeless refugees in exile.

In time, after Herod had died, they returned to the hill country around Nazareth where Jesus prepared for his coronation. But that was later . . . and is an even more amazing account (although this one takes some beating).

So, Christmas is all about miracles and dreams and angels, but most of all it is about a King. But no ordinary King. A King whose entire wealth consists of us. Because Jesus the King sees us, as treasure beyond worth. We are the King's delight . . .

Now that is worth a pile of celebrations.

The Sweet News of Christmas...

it's all here in this exciting new telling of the edible, incredible and sustaining joy that is Christmas.

Written by **Stewart Henderson** and **J. John,** The Sweet News of Christmas brings the flavour and fullness of the Nativity to children and adults alike.

Go on, spoil yourselves ... it's a stocking crammed with wonders ... it's a hamper of delights ... but, most of all, it's a manger where we begin to celebrate ...

ISBN 1-86024-234-0